DONALD TRUMP
AND THE WAR ON THE
"SILENT ENEMY"

RHONDA RIVERA

WESTBOW
PRESS®
A DIVISION OF THOMAS NELSON
& ZONDERVAN

WestBow Press books may be ordered through booksellers or by contacting:

WestBow Press
A Division of Thomas Nelson & Zondervan
1663 Liberty Drive
Bloomington, IN 47403
www.westbowpress.com
844-714-3454

ISBN: 978-1-6642-4539-6 (sc)
ISBN: 978-1-6642-4541-9 (hc)
ISBN: 978-1-6642-4540-2 (e)

Library of Congress Control Number: 2021919463

Print information available on the last page.

WestBow Press rev. date: 10/04/2021

CONTENTS

DEDICATION

I dedicate this book and its contents to all the COVID-19 families who have suffered in this pandemic. My vision is to see the proceeds go to providing Bibles to the victims and their families. I also would like to thank my president, Donald J. Trump, for protecting our country from all "silent enemies." He has a heart that beats red, white, and blue with a true patriot spirit to keep us all safe from harm. I am so thankful for my friends, teachers, family, and faith leaders who encouraged me to continue. This is a personal war for me as I suffer attacks from this silent enemy. I persevere in my own life with health issues from this intruder and in my personal walk with the Lord Jesus Christ. May all who read this book be shielded from the attacks of this silent, evil enemy, and I pray the Lord will place a shield of protection around us all!

INTRODUCTION

I begin with prayer as I bring the reader into this understanding of how we have a silent enemy—Satan—who though silent is very present. Dear Lord Jesus, may all who read this book understand that we are dealing with an enemy that continues to plague our nation. Father, help us to understand that the only way for You to be able to help us by remaining faithful and staying in prayer. The Bible tells us to remain in constant prayer, and if we do, You will hear us. Lord, our nation is in a pandemic, and the very gates of hell are trying to destroy the health of our nation through coronavirus 19. Lord, I want to thank our president, Donald J. Trump, and the faith leaders for their constant gathering to pray and seek Your face in this time of unrest and impending disaster. Lord, above all else, we acknowledge that You are the supreme ruler over all powers that plague our land. My earnest prayer throughout this book is to lead others to the understanding that You alone, Lord, are the One who can rewrite history and keep us safe until Your eminent return, and we will one day see no more wars or hear rumors of wars. Lord, as Your Holy Bible says in 2 Chronicles 7:14,[1] "If my people who are called by my name will humble themselves and pray and turn from their wicked ways, then will I hear from heaven and heal their land." Father, protect our president and all the faith leaders who are in this battle daily to stay strong and to remember that You are in this battle with us, and we will win.

1

Bibles and Prayers in Schools to Fend Off This Silent Enemy

I want us to understand the war Trump is going through and the role of the silent enemy concerning school and prayer. You may say, "Oh, come on, there is no silent enemy in war. War is war." Well I am here to let you know that we must not be caught off guard. We must look to our Creator in this battle and see the enemy who is in the battle with us. His very nature is to remain silent and hidden as he approaches to attack. Dr. David Jeremiah, senior pastor of the Shadow Mountain Church in California, helps us to pray a warriors' prayer and teaches us how to pray with Ephesians 6. This strong faith leader reminds us, "The armor of God is what we use to defend ourselves when Satan attacks. It is the warrior's uniform given to every Christian. It is composed of supernatural tools He has given us to contend with the rulers of a dark and imperfect world."[2] Dr. Jeremiah has written many books on how to fight the battle against the silent enemy.

Have you read Joyce Meyer's book *The Battlefield of the Mind*? She opens the introduction with the importance of our thoughts in dealing with the silent enemy. She uses Proverbs 23:7: "For as he [a person] thinks in his heart so is he."[3] She warns us to watch our words and thoughts. You see, the devil controls our minds in subtle ways. We must remember 2 Corinthians 10:4–5 (NLT):

> For the weapons of our warfare are not physical [weapons of flesh and blood], but they are mighty before God for the overthrow and destruction of strongholds, [in as much as we] refute arguments and theories and reasoning's and every proud and lofty thing that sets itself up against the [true] knowledge of God; and we lead every thought and purpose away

captive unto the obedience of Christ (the Messiah, the Anointed One).[4]

Lord, help us to defeat the silent enemy in our minds by hiding scripture in our hearts. Lord, help this strong faith leader to remain strong and keep the devil from her mind so she can help others fight this battle.

Harvest Ministries and Greg Laurie remind us to stand strong through Satan's attacks. This pastor uses Ephesians 6:10 to show that we should, "Be strong in the Lord and the power of His might,"[5] when we fight against this schemer. He argues we are no match for the devil. He includes in his message that Satan is a powerful spiritual entity who cannot be dealt with on our own. Most of all, don't lose your faith, and rely on your past battles when God shows up. Jesus promises us that God is greater and is holding us. The next scripture, he explains, will help us as we are being tested. We must remember the words of Jesus in John 10:29, as paraphrased from the King James Version: My Father is greater than all, and no one can snatch them out of my Fathers hand.[6] And Romans 8:38–39 confirms that absolutely nothing will separate us from the love of God in Christ Jesus.[7] You see, the silent enemy, Satan, doesn't want us to know that he was defeated at the cross. First John 3:8 explains, "For this purpose the Son of Man was manifested, that He might destroy the works of the devil."[8] Colossians 2:14 and John 12:31–32 give us more insight into the significance of the Lord's power breaking through. Jesus broke the stranglehold that Satan had on humanity when he died on the cross.[9] Thank you, Greg, for reminding us about John 10:29: "My Father is greater than all; and no one is able to snatch them out of My Father's hand."[10]

Where is the silent part when Satan tries to separate us from the heart of God? He tries to render us defenseless when we fight by ourselves without God's help. So don't you think we should let the Lord aid us in this battle? You ask, how do we do this? I tell you the key to stopping the enemy is what we do in the battle. We must rely on God and pray. And we must teach our children to pray and read the Bible so that they can use it to defend against the devil. I believe the greatest part of the message that Greg is trying to portray in his message to us is not to worry because this silent enemy was taken down at the cross. First John 3:8 says, "For this purpose the son of God was manifested, that He might destroy the works of the devil."[11] Remember, we are not in this alone; we have God to help us and our families. We must always look to Him and stay close to our Bibles to defeat the enemy.

Please, all faith leaders and fellow citizens, pray for Trump and our country in every hour. Why do we need to pray? Well let me tell you, we can reach the very throne of God when we do what the Bible says. Trump established and reinstituted guidelines for prayer in public schools on January 16, 2020.[12] He also signed a bill allowing the Bible in schools and events on January 28, 2019.[13] This enabled all to worship freely their Creator with the freedom that this nation was founded on since the first Pilgrims landed on Plymouth Rock. The Pilgrims sailed from England to Plymouth Rock, in what is now Massachusetts, to be able to worship freely our Creator God without the Church of England telling them they could not do this, thereby binding them to the Church of England.[14] Dear friends, if you are a Christian, you are bound to no one but the Lord Jesus Christ, who suffered and died for us. We bear the cross of Christ with Jesus. Scripture tells us in Luke 9:23–24, "And he said to them all, if any man will come after me, let him deny himself, and take up his cross daily, and follow me."

How important is the Bible in the instructions of a parent? The guidance of a parent is likened to a lamp. Proverbs 6:23 illuminates: "For the commandment is a lamp; and the law is light; and the reproofs of instruction are the way of life." Lamps are symbols of guidance. Psalm 119:105–106 sheds light on the silent enemy's dark deeds:

Thy Word is a lamp unto my feet and a light unto my path. I have sworn and I will perform it, that I will keep thy judgment righteous.

Your very soul is the Lord's lamp. Proverbs 20:27 lights the way when it explains that the human spirit and the Holy Spirit intertwine as you read scripture. As a Christian, you see the manifestation of the Holy Spirit's activity: "The Spirit of man is the candle of the Lord, searching all the inward parts of the belly" (Proverbs 20:27).

The silent enemy comes to detour our efforts to honor Christ in our hearts and families. Who is that enemy but Satan himself? He comes to steal, kill, and destroy. If we are abiding in Christ and trying to share the good news of the gospel, Matthew 13:19 says, in the Christian Standard Bible (CSB) translation, "When anyone hears the word about the kingdom and doesn't understand it, the evil one comes and snatches away what was sown in his heart." So Satan is trying to stop everyone from sharing the message of God's love.

Lord Jesus, we pray that the Word of God will be established for whoever is reading this and will remain firm within their hearts so that Satan will not be able to steal what You have sown there.

The model prayer is given to us by the greatest teacher the world will ever know. Jesus Christ told His disciples to pray this prayer when they came up to Him in Luke 11 while He was praying. They asked for instruction. He replied with scripture as He always does in the Bible. Matthew 6:9–13 is the passage most Christians know so well as the Lord's Prayer. He taught us always to pray this prayer in our daily lives. In the Old English of the King James Version, it goes like this:

> After this manner therefore pray ye: Our Father which art in heaven, Hallowed be thy name. Thy kingdom come, Thy will be done in earth, as it is in heaven. Give us this day our daily bread. And forgive us our debts, as we forgive our debtors. And lead us not into temptation, but deliver us from evil: For thine is the kingdom, and the power, and the glory, for ever. Amen.

Lord, I pray this prayer of protection over the president, his staff, and the faith leaders of our nation and the COVID-19 victims' families and survivors in Jesus's holy name. Please, Lord, help keep us aware that we are under constant attack. Remember that God is with us in this spiritual battle. Second Corinthians 10:3–5 confirms, "For though we walk in the flesh, we do not war after the flesh: (For the weapons of our warfare are not carnal, but mighty through God to the pulling down of strong holds;) Casting down imaginations, and every high thing that exalteth itself against the knowledge of God, and bringing into captivity every thought to the obedience of Christ;" meaning God will fight and bring this silent enemy into submission.

We must teach our children how to grow in knowledge so that they may be prosperous in this world. God instructs us to keep the words of scripture close to their hearts, daily enabling them to be strong and faithful Christians standing strong against the enemy. Deuteronomy 11:20 (NIV) tells us to "write them on the doorframes of your houses and on your gates." You see how much the Lord wants us to seek His Word concerning knowledge? He wants us to teach our children to stay in the Holy Scriptures so that their roads will not be traveled alone, and it may even be easier to travel.

Dear Lord, help us to keep America faithful through our devotion time with You as we walk in this world with the Bible by our sides for guidance and instruction. We must adhere to scripture so that we may be able to defeat the devil and his schemes to divide our nation, which is firmly founded in God.

2

The Silent Enemy Is Present
in the Prolife Battle

What does the Bible say about killing the unborn child? You see, this started when Christ was born, and Revelation explains about the invisible enemy. His plan from the beginning was to kill our Messiah. His attacks continue on those believers who have accepted Him and trust Him to save them on the final day. Chapter 12 of Revelation speaks of the dragon who came to devour the child. The Roman Catholic Church believes the woman is Mary, but I stand with reformed theology that the woman represents the church. So you see, the devil is the silent enemy after the very souls of our children, especially the ones who profess faith in Jesus Christ. He wants to destroy the witnesses so we can't help others know of God's great love for humanity.

We, as Christian leaders and teachers, must remember that the Lord cherishes children. Psalm 127:3 reminds us that children are a, "heritage of the Lord and the fruit of the womb is his reward," and Jeremiah 1:5 (RSV) states, "Before I formed you in the womb I knew you, and before you were born I consecrated you; I appointed you a prophet to the nations." So you see, God has a plan for our lives as Christians. It is so important to keep our thoughts on the words of the Bible so we can keep America faithful as my vision and goal of this book and my ministry demands.

Another way the devil attacks us silently is by attacks on our unborn through the leaders who run our country. Thanks be to Donald J. Trump and Mike Pence, the devil's murderous schemes are being thwarted. You may wonder how they helped. Well, they instituted laws that help fight against allowing the ones whose eyes have been darkened to believe the lie that ending a life is okay in the sight of God. Second Corinthians 4:4 (NKJV) tells us, "Whose minds the god of this age has blinded, who do not believe, lest the light of the gospel of the glory of Christ, who is the image of God should shine on them." They participated in the prolife march that stands for protection of the unborn. Donald J. Trump and Mike Pence spoke at this event in remembrance of Nellie Gray, who had close to twenty thousand supporters on January 22, 1974. God is happy with this an event because it helps educate and lead our youth to stand for the unborn. This event prompted efforts to reverse the 1973 Supreme Court decision in *Roe v. Wade*, which legalized abortions. President Donald J. Trump honored this Gray, who founded the prolife march, in the National Garden of American Heroes.[15] The March for Life professes, "The Mission we embrace [is that] we promote the beauty and dignity of every human life by working to end abortion–by uniting, educating, and mobilizing pro-life people in the public square."[16] It is my prayer that all Christians join in this March for Life movement. Please go to the website marchforlife.org to help save lives of the unborn.

Thank God for all the judges who follow the Bible. Justice Brett Kavanaugh has a godly family and stands up for what is right in this country. Justice Kavanaugh, God bless you and your family for your faith witness. Sorry so many tried to stop you. I want to extend a personal thank you for those judges standing in the gap for the Lord and our country.

President Donald J. Trump shared his heart in the message and was profoundly honored to be the first president to attend the March for Life event. He invited his constituents to join him in this momentous event when he stated, "We are here for a very simple reason, to defend the right of every child born and unborn, to fulfill their God given potential. For 47 years Americans from all backgrounds of the country have come to stand for life."[17] He thanked the high school and college students who took long bus rides to be there that day in our nation's capital. Donald Trump emphasizes that young people are the hearts of the March for Life and that it is their generation that makes this nation pro-family and prolife. He acknowledges that this life movement is led by strong women, amazing faith leaders, and brave students who carry on the legacy of the pioneers who fought to raise the conscience of our nation and uphold the rights of our citizens. He adds that this group embraces mothers with care and compassion that come through prayer and unselfish love.[18]

Our God-fearing president thanks his constituents and continues by saying everyone attending understands that every child is a sacred gift from God: "Together we must protect the sanctity of every human life, and when we glimpse the image of a baby in the womb, we glimpse the majesty of God's creation, and when we hold a newborn in our arms, we know the love that each newborn brings to a family."[19] This faithful Christian leader explains that the value of seeing the child grow is of utmost importance. Our president reiterates, "We will see the splendor that each child radiates from each human soul, and this one life can change a whole family."[20] Our president emphasizes a great love. Trump swore from his first day in office to protect families and the unborn. He also wants to remove taxpayers from funding these atrocities.[21]

What is the president's stance on abortion globally? He stands strong against any policy and would veto any that encourages the destruction of human life. Globally he stood against any nation that would attack nations that attacked innocent lives. He claims that no one has made a stronger stance for this in the White House. He stands with God. He references the Bible when he says, "Each of us is wonderfully made."[22] (Psalm 139:14: "I will praise thee; for I am fearfully and wonderfully made: marvelous are thy works; and that my soul knoweth right well.") This leader stands for religious liberties and has fought all over the world and in this nation to protect even the Little Sisters of the Poor, which supports faith-based adoptions. This great leader states that left-wing politicians are trying to ban this movement for the sanctity of the right for life, but he will continue to fight for those who have no voice, and he claims we will win this battle.[23] The silent enemy will not have our children. Trump says together we are a voice for the voiceless.

Vice President Pence added a thanks to the president and his family for attending the forty-fourth annual March for Life event. Vice President Pence thought it was a good day, and he was deeply humbled to be the first vice president to attend. He quoted the Declaration of Independence, which states that all of us are, "endowed by [our] creator with certain inalienable rights and among these are life, liberty and the pursuit of happiness."[24] (The text of Declaration of Independence can be found at https://www.archives.gov/founding-docs/declaration-transcript.)[25] He stated that forty-four years ago, the Supreme Court turned away from these timeless ideals, but now, three generations later, people are standing for the unborn, and life is winning again. Pence emphasized that Trump wanted to be there to thank everyone for their compassion for the women and children of America. The vice president shared the Mexico City policy, which ends funding of organizations worldwide that promote abortions, and stops taxpayer funding while devoting those services to women across America.

Isn't it gratifying that Trump believes that a nation will be judged by how it treats the most vulnerable—the aged, the infirm?[26] Can you see how God uses our Christian leaders to work on defeating the silent enemy for His purposes on ending the death of the unborn?

We Christians search the news daily to find sources that will give us accurate information. I would like to thank those brave leaders who come to us in the news: Sean Hannity, Laura Ingram, and Bret and a few others. Also, I want to commend our "lone rangers," like Dan Bongino, who fight daily to reach the world with truth and strive to keep us informed of sincerity and accuracy in the news. Other faith leaders, such as Jeff Beck and Mark Levin of *Blaze News* and Judge Jeanine Pirro of *Justice with Judge Jeanine*, seek to give us truth, liberty, and honest validity. While other journalists turn their backs on moral ethics for money and prestige, these moral journalists and leaders forge through the media and mediocracies from the silent enemy that plague our land. They must read their Bibles and stay abreast of social events to keep on top of this important information. With God as their guide and His Word as their path, they are able to guide us through this injustice with the Lord's help. Pray for them as they are under direct attack.

I also commend Trump's cabinet members who stand beside him. And thank you, Kellyanne Conway, for your compassionate heart in helping advise him through many storms. I want to extend a special thanks to Mike Pompeo and his wife for their vision to provide support to children. Both are central figures trying to provide solace to Americans. They also travel to foreign soil to protect all

Americans. Please pray for our president and his family as they have recovered from the devastating COVID-19 virus. Also, remember the new press secretary, Kayleigh McEnany, as she is recovering from COVID-19.

Remember Jesus always comes to give us divine inspiration and life. He encourages us to press on in our battles to defeat the forces of darkness. Christ defeated Satan when He rose from the grave. We must remember the Lord gave us the Bible so we can know the end of the story, and Jesus Christ wins. You see now why it is so important to keep reading the Bible so we can be refreshed and nourished in the Word of God. You see, we are in a race, and Jesus is waiting for us at the end. Paul educates us about this in the book of Romans. I even wrote a song called "Marathon of Love" so we can understand to keep on pressing on to allow Christ to complete His work in us. The apostle Paul tells us to remain strong and hold on because a prize awaits faith leaders. Philippians 3:14 encourages us to do as Paul suggested: "I press toward the mark for the prize of the high calling of God in Christ Jesus."

3

———◦◦◦———

Trump and Pence Stay Dedicated to the Military Despite the Silent Enemy

The enemy's hidden agenda is to suppress the fact we are in a Christian battle. This silent enemy tries to stop our witnessing. I encourage all believers to stay strong and be good soldiers. Second Timothy describes this perfectly. Eunice and Lois taught Timothy well. Although he was young, they helped to build him up in the Lord. We need to encourage and build up our youth for they are the Joshuas of tomorrow and lead the way into the Promised Land. For a better understanding of the Joshua generation,

I encourage you to go to the following site, where there is a deeper understanding of this vision for our youth, the Joshua generation of the future: http://www.christcovenantcoalition. com/blog-entries/2017/2/6/7-powerful-traits-of-the-joshua-generation. See also Bishop Joseph Mattera's article "7 Powerful Traits of the Joshua Generation."[27] Why is this scripture as important as a soldier in the army of the Lord? Because we must not forget who gives us the strength to fight all battles. Second Timothy 2:2–3 (NLT) empowers us to "endure suffering along with me as a good soldier of Christ Jesus." These strong Christian women say to him, "Timothy my dear son, be strong through the grace that God gives you in Christ Jesus" (2 Timothy 2:1 NLT). Teach these truths to trustworthy people who will be able to pass them on to others. We must embrace the shield of faith and remember that we are righteous by our faith. As Christian soldiers, we are moving from faith to greater faith. Ephesians 6:16 (RSV) states, "Besides all these, [take] the shield of faith, with which you can quench all the flaming darts of the evil one." We can defeat this silent enemy by applying our faith in the Lord Jesus Christ and His promises found in the Holy Bible. "You will keep him in perfect peace, whose mind is stayed on you, because he trusts in You. Trust in the Lord forever, for in YAH the Lord, is everlasting strength" (Isaiah 26:3–4 NKJV).

Here is one example of our leaders using their Christian values to help our men in arms. President Trump and Vice President Pence have visited and supported our nation's soldiers to provide comfort to them on the battlefield. One account tells of them standing in the rain to support the fallen soldiers, which took place on February 11, 2020. After a rally in New Hampshire, they stopped at Dover Air Force Base to take part in a dignified transfer ceremony of two twenty-eight-year-old soldiers killed in Afghanistan. There was talk about Trump only caring for the elite of our country, but he showed others he cares for our soldiers who died preserving our liberty.[28]

I encourage all leaders that when they are under attack from this silent enemy to remember to think about good things to help their souls. Philippians 4:8 helps soldiers tremendously, stating, "Finally, brethren, whatsoever things are true, whatsoever things are honest, whatsoever things are just, whatsoever things are pure, whatsoever things are lovely, whatsoever things are of good report; if there be any virtue, and if there be any praise, think on these things." Trump and Pence held a brief prayer inside a C-17 plane and then stood at attention in the rain as the two caskets were carried out.[29] This is a stellar example of compassion for the families of the fallen soldiers and their families helping us keep America faithful as we care for those who fight hard for our freedom in this country.

4

Recognition of Holidays Concerning
Christ Jesus and How the Silent
Enemy Wants to Stop Us

W hy do we recognize the holidays for our Lord and
Savior Jesus Christ? Because the Bible tells us to
continue daily until the Lord returns. Trump truly wanted
the nation to reopen from the pandemic-caused lockdown so
that people could worship and attend their churches. Sadly,
the silent enemy was not done wreaking havoc in our nation
and throughout the world. Trump addressed the nation
through his Twitter account and spoke about Palm Sunday.

He tweeted the importance of this holiday, which was screen captured on the blog of Pastor Greg Laurie. Trump's tweet read, "Palm Sunday is the beginning of Holy Week for many people of Faith and a great day to lift our voices in prayer."[30] Trump let the world know that he would be listening to Pastor Greg Laurie of the Harvest Church in Riverside, California.[31] This is a link to hear from this pastor with the worldwide outreach who has a strong heart for the message of Jesus Christ: www.harvest.org. You see, the silent enemy wants to stop us from being a nation that praises the Lord God Almighty. We need to stay united in prayer so we can divert the enemy's plans.

The Christian Broadcasting Network (CBN) acknowledged President Trump as he held a prayer meeting with Bishop Harry Jackson. This news source reports Trump's convictions: "We place our trust in the hands of Almighty God."[32] On Good Friday, Trump participates with Bishop Harry Jackson from Hope Christian Church in Beltsville, Maryland. Trump explains, "As our nation battles the invisible enemy, we reaffirm that Americans believe in the power of prayer. We give thanks to the majesty of creation and for the gift of eternal life and we place our trust in the hands of Almighty God."[33] He continues to console: "At this time we pray that God will heal the sick and comfort the broken hearted and bless our heroes."[34]

Are you beginning to see who the silent enemy is and how he operates? Well if not, it is Satan himself. This fallen, angelic enemy of God must go before the throne of God to ask to attack each of us.

> Now there was a day when the sons of God came to present themselves before the Lord, and Satan came also among them. And the Lord said unto Satan, "Whence comest thou?" Then Satan answered the Lord, and said, "From going to and fro in the earth, and from walking up and down in it." And the Lord said unto Satan, "Hast thou considered my servant Job, that there is none like him in the earth, a perfect and an upright man, one that feareth God, and escheweth evil?" Then Satan answered the Lord, and said, "Doth Job fear God for nought? Hast not thou made an hedge about him, and about his house, and about all that he hath on every side? Thou hast blessed the work of his hands, and his substance is increased in the land." (Job 1:6–10)

Then the devil told the Lord that if he allowed him to strike Job, as the story continues, that he would curse the

Lord. Sadly, the Lord allowed Satan to do damage, and Job lost his children. Job went through many horrible things after God's protection was taken off him. His friends turned their backs on him, and his wife questioned him, but Job still did not curse God for all he lost.

Scholars have several speculations about why God spoke to Job. I believe God wanted Job to realize He held all the wisdom. God told him, "Who is this that obscures my words without knowledge? Brace yourself like a man and you shall answer me, where were you when I laid the earths foundation? Tell me if you understand who marked off its dimensions? Surely you know! Who stretched a measuring line across it? On what were its footings set, or who laid its cornerstone" (Job 38:1–6 NIV). The Lord continues to ask Job about all He created and all He provided for. I pray that those who read this book will go to their Bibles and read the whole story.

After God spoke to Job about all this, He asked him, "'Shall he that contends with the Almighty instruct him? He that reproves God, let him answer it.' Then Job answered the Lord and said, 'Behold I am vile. What shall I answer you? I will lay my hand upon my mouth'" (Job 42:2–4). He continues by telling the Lord that He has spoken to him of things that he did not understand. He repented and told the Lord that he despised himself. Now the Lord was pleased with Job because He didn't curse Him, and Job answered with humility.

As the Bible story unfolds, the Lord speaks to Eliphaz the Temanite and is angry with him and his two friends because the truth was not spoken about Him. This is where the silent enemy attacks all believers that they may not know the truth about the Lord. Do you believe it, after they were so horrible to Job, he still prayed for his friends, and God restored Job and gave him twice his fortunes and gave him a long life?

Lord, I am asking You to please help us to understand where the silent enemy tries to attack us. We want always to hear the truth concerning You; and as faith leaders and teachers, we want to do this correctly. Please stay with us, Lord, and guide us to do Your will. This is our earnest prayer. In Jesus's holy name we pray, Amen.

5

———◦◦◦◦———

Preserving and Protecting Israel and the Jewish Nation against the Silent Enemy

Why is it important to protect Israel and the Jewish nation? As a Christian nation, we, as leaders in the faith, are commanded to protect the Jews and Israel. America should protect this tiny country that the Lord loves so much. Those who are students of the sacred scriptures and with an understanding of the Bible realize God has protected these people throughout history. Jesus was a Jew and practiced all the Jewish traditions. History concludes that God delivered

His people during the exodus from Egypt to the Promised Land. This is a great story; you must tell your children how God provided for His people. I remember being in Sunday school, which reminds me that as we embrace other beliefs, we should do it in the manner that Paul instructed the church in Ephesus. He said we are to embrace others with love and compassion.

How does the silent enemy stop us from doing this? By trying to move us to take on our enemies on our own without the help of the Lord. If we allow the Lord to fight our battles, we can rest in the assurance that He will bring restitution to us in the event that we are under attack. Paul instructs us to love each other. It is God's greatest commandment. Scripture reminds us in Matthew 22:36–40, "'Master, which is the great commandment in the law?' Jesus said unto him 'Thou shalt love the Lord with all thy heart, with all thy soul, and with all thy mind. This is the first and great commandment. And the second is like unto it. Thou shalt love thy neighbor as thyself. On these two commandments hang all the law and the prophets.'"

Dr. Billy Graham had to be one of the greatest voices for the Lord this nation and the world have ever seen. His son and grandson, Franklin Graham and Will Graham, respectively, and other family members are helping others in many ways. One way Franklin is helping so many people is through Samaritan's Purse, the organization that helps worldwide. Franklin Graham even went directly to the COVID-19 victims and risked his life, along with Michael W. Smith, to proclaim the gospel message of Christ in New York City's Central Park.[35] Thank you, Michael W. Smith, for singing "Waymaker."[36] Lord, You will surely will make a way. These are mighty warriors of the faith, along with nurses and doctors who bravely press on though this silent enemy and his attack when their lives are on the line for our great nation.

My daughter and I were blessed to work for Dr. Billy Graham at the Cove for four years. We helped many evangelists, missionaries, and leaders. If you aren't familiar with the Cove, this is a retreat center where people come to learn and be trained. This oasis brings deep spiritual revival and much needed time alone with the Lord. Dr. Billy Graham speaks of Jesus's love and how it conquers negative attitudes in response to a question asked him as posted in "Answers" on the Billy Graham Evangelistic Association website. The writer wrote about a person who claims to be a Christian but is always negative and critical. The question asked if Jesus was like this. Dr. Graham answered with several passages, including Mark 12:37. This is an exciting passage. The crowd listened to hear Jesus's reply concerning positive affirmations. Instead of damaging someone with negativism, and damage their faith, a positive message is given. Dr. Graham explained to the writer that Jesus was not critical like this: "instead of putting people down, He sought to win them over by His love and compassion" ("Begin Your Journey to Peace" at PeaceWithGod.Net).[37] On one occasion, the Bible says, "The large crowd listened to him with delight" (Mark 12:37). This doesn't mean Jesus refused to rebuke those who were doing wrong, not at all. In fact, some of His strongest words were directed at those who distorted God's Word and were only interested in their own power or positions. But even then, His message was one of forgiveness and hope if they would only repent and open their hearts to Him.

He reminds us that Christ came not only to take us to heaven someday but also to fill our hearts with love. Dr. Billy Graham also emphasizes the deep importance of loving all when he paraphrases 2 John 6: As you have heard from the beginning his command is that you walk in love.[38]

Faith leaders, how does the silent enemy of our souls distract us from helping others? Well, he uses lies when he wants us to become great within our own merit. This is a lie of the devil. We have no merit; we as Christians rely on the substitutionary death and unmerited love of Jesus Christ and what He can accomplish through us. I pray that we remain faithful and can truly help others to keep America faithful.

As Christian leaders, we must keep the understanding that the Lord is the One fighting for us. We don't want to be so full of ourselves that Christ can't enter our hearts and keep us close to Him for protection from a silent attack. We must stay humble and allow the Lord to change us into His likeness. His likeness is much better than ours. Second Corinthians 3:18 says, "But we all, with open face beholding as in a glass the glory of the Lord, are changed into the same image from glory to glory, even as by the Spirit of the Lord."

You know the silent enemy doesn't know love at all. He is just a fallen angel who wants to be God, so he uses any means to fool us in to believing his lies and deceptions. We can defeat this silent enemy by using love. Ephesians 4:2 tells us to act, "with all lowliness and meekness, and longsuffering, forbearing one another in love." We are urged to be in one mind and spirit as we accomplish this together for the honor of the Lord Jesus Christ. Confirmation is found in this passage:

> Finally, be ye all of one mind, having compassion one of another, love as brethren, be pitiful, be courteous: Not rendering evil for evil, or railing for railing: but contrariwise blessing; knowing that ye are thereunto called, that ye should inherit a blessing. For

he that will love life, and see good days, let him refrain his tongue from evil, and his lips that they speak no guile: Let him eschew evil, and do good; let him seek peace, and ensue it. (1 Peter 3:8–11)

Lord Jesus, help us to always rely on You and Your power concerning enemies or those who don't fully understand Your love and Your message of redemption. Help us as faithful leaders and teachers to rely on You and Your promises when dealing with those who are lost.

6

The First Lady and Her Acts of
Compassion for the American
People Despite the Silent Enemy

Second Corinthians 5:20 (NKJV) states, "Now then, we are ambassadors for Christ, as though God were pleading through us: we implore you on Christ's behalf, be reconciled to God." The first lady is always ridiculed and brought down by this silent enemy. Melania Trump is always judged for her career in modeling, but she is a beautiful woman who loves the Lord and lives a quiet lifestyle. She always reflects a godly mother as she takes care of her son,

Barron. She shields him from the media so he can live a regular life as much as possible. Lord, I pray for our first lady. May You continue to keep her at peace as she guides her family in Your ways. Lord, keep her versed on Your Word so the silent enemy will not attack her family or efforts to help the ones she has vowed to help.

Melania Trump must be commended for her Be Best program, which focuses on well-being for youth and advocates against cyberbullying and drug (particularly opioid) abuse. WhiteHouse.Gov recognizes her as she has expanded her goal to educating children and parents about the issues they face and to promoting programs and services available to help them with today's challenges. She has added twenty-two ambassadors to her program and visited Africa and Egypt to help globally. She is a true Christian with a heart for helping others. She has met with thousands of children who suffer and has met with major technological companies to practice digital civility. In her own words, "I am thrilled that we have identified and partnered with so many organizations, both inside and outside of government, to help promote and expand the three pillars of Be Best." She continues, "As we move into the next phase of my initiative, I look forward to the work ahead. There is no greater opportunity than that of helping children reach their fullest potential as they grow up."[39]

7

Second Lady Karen Pence and
Her Work with Military Spouses
Despite the Silent Enemy

T he silent enemy has not given this godly teacher an easy road to travel. He continually tries to attack her efforts to help others in their faith. Lord, I am praying on her behalf that You stop any efforts of the silent enemy, so she can do the work You have for her to fulfill. *The Jacksonville Daily News* reports, "Second Lady Pence visits camp Lejeune, offers support to military families. In the fall of 2018."[40] Pence traveled and launched an awareness campaign to promote and encourage military spouses and employment challenges.[41] Donald Trump offers his advice for them to look for employment in the federal government. Pence held two White House summits with more than fifty companies on the topic. The Pences have a son who is a marine and a daughter who is a navy aviator, and they encourage them to take pride in their work. It is very dear to the second lady's heart to help reduce red tape and enable servicemembers to find work that requires state licensing.[42]

Lord, thank You for all the sacrifices that the second lady has made while serving in the White House on behalf of the American people. Father, keep the second lady strong and safe from any upcoming attacks as she moves forward in her efforts to secure the American people and military spouses.

8

Donald Trump, Mike Pence, the
COVID-19 Task Force, and the
War on the Silent Enemy

The Trump administration is fully aware of the silent
enemy that plagues our nation. Every day the president
and his cabinet have to ward off attacks from the news media
and political opponents who do not have the best interests of
Americans in their minds. The president, vice president, and
the cabinet know where to run, and they ask many faithful
ministers and Christians to take part in this prayerful fight.
President Trump and Vice President Pence go straight to the

cabinet room and pray on many occasions. There is even a presidential prayer channel. Will you also be a part of this prayer channel to help them ward off the attacks of this silent enemy? If so, go to http://PresidentialPrayerTeam.org and become a part of this team in taking down the wiles of this silent enemy and helping to keep America faithful.

The White House Coronavirus Task Force was organized February 26, 2020. Mike Pence was named chair of the task force, and Deborah Birx was named the response coordinator.[43] The first case in America was a thirty-five-year-old man who returned from Wuhan, China, on January 15, 2020.[44] The World Health Organization declared a national emergency, and the Trump administration restricted travel on entry from those from China.[45] On March 10, 2020, Republican senators encouraged President Trump to make Anthony Fauci the face of the federal government's COVID-19 response because Fauci was credible and spoke with authority in the medical community.[46] Trump made nursing homes and patients priorities. He and his administration distributed $333 million to help nursing homes during the pandemic curb deaths and infections in this vulnerable population hit so hard by the virus.[47]

The task force's briefings inform the citizens about COVID-19 in their states and tells us to listen to our state officials for instructions as we try to curb the pandemic.

Pray for them as they try to find remedies and medicines to help all American citizens fight and survive this horrible pandemic. Please pray for all those who continue to battle COVID-19, and for President Trump and others of both past and present administrations who continue to heal from this disease.

Dear leaders, listen to the heart of Charles Stanley. This pastor from *In Touch* ministries is a very well-seasoned pastor who has weathered many storms and has a voice from God's own heart. He tells us to stay strong. "Fear thou not; for I am with thee: be not dismayed; for I am thy God: I will strengthen thee; yea, I will help thee, I will uphold thee with the right hand of my righteous" (Isaiah 41:10).

> I recommend that believers underline Isaiah 41 in their Bible and meditate on it frequently. When one of God's people is seeking an anchor in turbulent times, this is the right passage for the job. Here, Isaiah writes about the source of Christians' strength.
>
> In Isaiah 41:10 alone, the Lord promises strength, help, and protection. Moreover, He gives two commands: "Do not fear" and "Do not anxiously look about you." Among Satan's subtle and successful traps is the art

of distraction. The evil one knows that fear can choke faith. He works hard to make unsettling circumstances a person's sole focus. Once a believer's attention is diverted from God, natural human tendencies take over. In the absence of prayer and worship, anxiety and doubt grow unobstructed.

Staying focused on the Lord can be hard. The flesh prefers to seek security by thinking through all possible angles. Our tendency is to weigh what we think could happen against what "experts" say will happen, and then to evaluate possible ways of preventing our worst fears from coming true. Instead of becoming more confident, we begin to realize how powerless we are. Thankfully, we serve an almighty God who says, "Surely I will help you" (Isaiah 41:10). We can count on Him.

By focusing on our circumstances, we're actually choosing to feel anxiety and doubt, but these emotions don't belong in a believer's daily life. Instead, let's decide to trust in the promises God has given us. He has filled His Word with scriptural anchors to keep His children steady in the faith.[48]

I believe that as we anchor and saturate ourselves in God's Word, we are reminded that the Lord is faithful to sustain us. Let's be reassured that when the silent enemy comes to dampen our faith in the storms of life, Christ promises to be with us.

Another great voice to hear from is Dr. Tony Evans from Oak Cliff Bible Fellowship in Dallas, Texas. He encourages us to apply Matthew 6:25–33:

> Therefore I say unto you, Take no thought for your life, what ye shall eat, or what ye shall drink; nor yet for your body, what ye shall put on. Is not the life more than meat, and the body than raiment?
>
> Behold the fowls of the air: for they sow not, neither do they reap, nor gather into barns; yet your heavenly Father feedeth them. Are ye not much better than they?
>
> Which of you by taking thought can add one cubit unto his stature?
>
> And why take ye thought for raiment? Consider the lilies of the field, how they grow; they toil not, neither do they spin:

And yet I say unto you, That even Solomon in all his glory was not arrayed like one of these.

Wherefore, if God so clothe the grass of the field, which today is, and tomorrow is cast into the oven, shall he not much more clothe you, O ye of little faith?

Therefore take no thought, saying, What shall we eat? or, What shall we drink? or, Wherewithal shall we be clothed?

(For after all these things do the Gentiles seek:) for your heavenly Father knoweth that ye have need of all these things.

But seek ye first the kingdom of God, and his righteousness; and all these things shall be added unto you.

Dr. Tony Evans indicates that we are reaching out to leaders, and we are all confused. He was in Las Vegas teaching a Bible study when the pandemic hit. Dr. Evans was trying to figure stuff out on the run while teaching the Word of God. He urged Christians to stay safe and trust God's provisions in this panicked condition. He relates, "We get into situations like this; it hits us and everyone around us." He encourages us to reach out to others in our families during a crisis and see that they are okay. Dr. Evans expresses legitimate concern about our fears. He explains that yes, we should be responsible, but worry is when it controls us. He argues, "Worry is concerned gone haywire. It tells you can't sleep, it dictates you, and makes you go into illegitimate worry." Dr. Tony Evans paraphrases Matthew 6:3. He prescribed and pounds home his illustration, "These are times not to worry, but your father or your daddy and his care in the midst of crisis brings a calming sense in your emotions and brings down fear." Dr. Evans explains that God is speaking to our world, which has wandered too far. This is a faith crisis. He encourages that crises like these cause us to care. He says, "It creates the absence of what crisis didn't do that God wants us to adjust in our life. Encouragement to reach out to others who need things to aid in any way possible was displayed." Dr. Evans focuses on the relational aspect of you and the Lord when he replies, "Don't worry because you have a daddy, and you may have to adjust your life on a dime." Continuing, "Remember it's a time to be concerned but not to worry" (see https://youtu.be/TO9Z8XL3M0k).[49]

Lord, as this silent enemy is trying to attack our confidence in You, let us rest assured You are with us, and You will bring us through this pandemic.

I was fortunate to meet Dr. Evans and his wife one day when I worked for Thomas Nelson Bible Publishing. They were speaking to all employees. It was an uplifting experience to meet with one of the pastors who was also one of our widely acclaimed authors.

I want you to know that the president's team is working endlessly to try to get a vaccine or any method available to end this horrific pandemic. We need to remain in prayer throughout the country as the Lord fights with us in warding off this silent enemy and bringing our nation back to health.

Lord, help our country to grow again and prosper as it did before the pandemic hit. Lord, our earnest prayer as faith leaders is to see our country back to work safely. We pray that everyone will honor You with their lives and testimony so that You can be glorified as Your Holy Word instructs us. Lord, keep the doctors and medical teams well, and help us to find the remedy to this horrible COVID-19. Lord, grant us wisdom on how to comfort the country. We truly want to be, "One nation under God." We acknowledge You are the only one who can stop this silent enemy from destroying our nation.

I encourage you to practice the presence of Jesus in your daily life to defeat the silent enemy." In his book, *Unmerited Favor*, Pastor Joseph Prince explains in chapter 17, "Becoming an Heir of the World," how we see the end of the devil's influence over us:

See The End of the Devil's Influence Over You

Do you know that the moment the blessing of Abraham is activated in a believer's life, the devil's influence over him is over? Now, imagine then, if you were the devil. What strategy would you use, knowing that the promise that a believer would be an heir of the world comes not through the law, but through the righteousness of faith? You would, of course, promote the law as much as possible, and transform all your demons into marketers and advertisers of the law. God's Word tells us that "Satan himself transforms himself into an angel of light. Therefore it is no great thing if his ministers also transform themselves into ministers of righteousness, whose end will be according to their works." And you wouldn't stop there. You would launch an all-out attack against the message of righteousness by faith, and at the same time, attempt to assassinate the reputation of those who preach this message. You would do all that you can to short-circuit and sabotage the very channel by which God releases the promise that believers would be heirs of the world.

My friend, open your eyes to the devil's devices and don't allow yourself to be robbed anymore! When the Lord first opened my eyes to the gospel of grace years ago, I really felt that I had been cheated in my Christian walk. It is so clear in the Bible and yet, I had suffered for years because of wrong believing. How I wish someone had taught me about the truths that I rejoice in today, truths like I am righteous by faith in Jesus and not by my own works! The law is about doing, whereas faith is about speaking. By the way, it is important that you know that righteousness by faith is not a "basic teaching." No, it is a powerful one. And even if you think that you already know all about this teaching, I challenge you to take a closer look at the areas of your life where the blessing of Abraham seems to be void and of no effect. I challenge you to really take time to look at those areas and ask yourself this question: "Do I really understand righteousness by faith?" I also want to challenge you to start speaking your righteousness by faith in those areas.[50]

Lord, as we understand the devices of the enemy, let us focus on Jesus Christ, the "commander and chief" of our lives. He will keep us safe through our belief in our righteousness by faith. Lord, may all the president's cabinet understand that we, as faith leaders, must instruct and guide others. The main focal point to remember is that Jesus Christ is Lord, and if we lean on Him, He will safely guide us and heal our land until the time we stand before Him. May we all be found faithful on Your return is my humble prayer.

9

The Silent Enemy Wants to
Stop the Word of God

I want to thank Donald J. Trump for one of the most heroic events in history. He successfully obtained the release Pastor Andrew Brunson from a Turkish prison. Pastor Brunson was a well-known pastor from my hometown of Black Mountain, North Carolina. If you are not familiar with his story, he was falsely accused of espionage when all he was doing was putting biblical material out to the public. He was arrested after serving in ministry in Turkey for twenty years and imprisoned for two years. Praise the

Lord, he said he wasn't abused or hurt while in prison, but he shared that this was one of the darkest battles of his life. In *Decision Magazine*, a publication of the Billy Graham Evangelistic Association—which I so love and was humbled to be a part of—shares the story in the December 2018 in an article titled, "I Knew God Wouldn't Forget Me: Andrew and Norine Brunson Tell How God Sustained Them During Andrew's Two Years in Prison." Brunson says it was all the prayers that truly sustained him while he was imprisoned.[51] You see, faith leaders, how prayer stopped the silent enemy in his footsteps? Thank you, Mr. President, for caring for the Lord's ministers and bringing them home from prison.

Lord, please stop the silent enemy. Father, as Your Word goes out, keep our faith leaders and missionaries safe in this dark hour that falls upon our nation.

10

Faith Leaders' Quests to Help
Us against the Silent Enemy

I sn't it great that we don't have to walk this path alone and
that we have Jesus? Well it's even more amazing that we
have faith leaders to help guide us too! I love my brothers and
sisters in the Lord. Two amazing brothers in Christ are the
Hagee men, who are in Texas. If you get a chance, stop by
and visit them; they will love you. Just remember when we
are in the storm and the silent enemy decides to prowl, we
are not alone. I was reading Pastor Hagee's *Storm Proof,* in
which he is trying to soothe us and help us understand that

with Jesus, we can survive the storm. We just need to go to the source, which is Jesus who will fight for us against this silent enemy. In his book, John Hagee describes that you can turn your storms into victories with this one hundred-day devotional. "God knew you were going through the storm long before you knew it was going to happen." He continues, "You never know how good God is until he rescues you from the storm."[52]

I'm here to tell you that we have a president who is constantly in a storm, fighting for our liberty as one nation under God to honor and pray and read our Bibles in schools and public places. Who can ask for more than that? We need to pray for our leaders. On page 129 of this devotional book, Hagee reminds us to look to David, who wrote the Psalms.[53] David knew who to run to, as evidenced in Psalm 27:1–3 (NIV) "The Lord is my light and my salvation—whom shall I fear? The Lord is the stronghold of my life—of whom shall I be afraid? When the wicked advance against me to devour me, it is my enemies and foes who will stumble and fall. Though an army besiege me, my heart will not fear; though war break out against me, even then I will be confident."

Before I go to scripture, I hope everyone will Satan-proof their homes. I remember being a young mother with three kids and no husband or man to help me. I depended on the church to help my children. I was also very close to the Lord at this time, and I had nowhere to turn but God. I bring this up because we are in a storm of life with this pandemic and running scared. I can tell you that the Lord always provided for my family. I moved back to North Carolina with my children. I remember a pastor who taught in the homeless shelter as part of a downtown ministry in Nashville. It was a big ministry, but he left it to help my family. He walked into my small home and felt something was not right. He sensed in my daughter's room a presence that was not right. Tom prayed to remove any evil that might be in my home. It touched my heart for someone to pray over my home. Well, my friends, there is the silent enemy that wants to take over your home. Pray the devil out. I say all this because in times of crisis, I listen to all faith leaders in the land.

One leader who touched my heart was Marilyn Hickey of Marilyn Hickey Ministries (https://www.marilynandsarah. org/).[54] She wrote a book called *Satan Proof Your Home*. She gives us specific instruction how to use the Word of God. "This hard hitting book unveils Satan's most subtle devices and gives you practical counsel. After reading this book, you'll know how to Satan proof yourself and those you love, stopping Satan dead in his tracks!"[55]

I enjoy reading the King James Version of the Bible because I believe it is a literary masterpiece. It was widely read for years but is now sometimes forgotten. You can read different versions, but I still prefer this version since this is what I read when I was growing up, and it speaks to my heart.

Do you know that the Holy Spirit is a person? Yes, it is the third part of the Godhead. The triune God exists in three persons: God the Father, Jesus the Son, and the Holy Spirit as Comforter. This part of God is given to believers when they accept and give their lives to Christ. This helper comes alongside us and helps us in our fight against the silent enemy. The Holy Spirit will illuminate our hearts and minds as we read God's Word. He teaches us in the way that we should go. You can find scriptures that explain the work of the Holy Spirit in our lives at https://dailyverses.net/spirit/kjv.[56]

Lord, as we listen to each other in the land and draw from Your teachings as faith leaders, help us to hear Your instructions and to stay close so we can guide others so the silent enemy can't hurt our witnessing. Lord, help us as we seek Your will in our land so that it can truly be said we are keeping America faithful.

Max Lucado is a faith leader and pastor at Oak Hill Church in San Antonio, Texas. He is at home during this pandemic and gives us a celebration of hope. He reminds us that one day we will be together again to worship. He claims we are worried and have unease. He explains that we might miss an event, but through this crisis, we are together in a spirit of unity. He said he doesn't like wearing a mask because it makes him look like a bank robber. So he decided not to wear one while shopping at a nearby store. This pastor was humbled when he saw a mom and kids and health worker wearing masks. He came to the realization that we are going through this together as a nation.

Pastor Lucado was sent a song from Steven Curtis Chapman that he loved and shared it on a podcast. I love Steven also. I met him at a youth conference in Atlanta with my college colleagues from Montreat College during my undergrad. Steven Curtis Chapman is a humble Christian artist with a desire to reach the world through his music. The song Steven sent was "We Will Get through This Together."

Max Lucado shares the unity as a colorful experience. He shares that we must remember 9/11 with all its flags and national awareness. There must be a season of unity. The message is that we are all in this together. He uses the message of the Lord's Supper. He does this with all online media. He, like Trump, wants us to be as one in this country and well through this pandemic.[57]

11

The Silent Enemy and How to
Defeat Satan with Scripture

As we "pray God's Word back to Him,"[58] we find that
the silent enemy has to leave because forces of evil
must leave when truth is going out. This is the key to keeping
America faithful. Our faith, hope, and trust are hidden in our
hearts through God's Word, and we will win the battle. As
you battle against this silent enemy, find strength from these
selected verses of scripture taken from Debbie McDaniel's
article, "31 Spiritual Warfare Scriptures: Help for Facing
Life's Battles:"[59]

- "Be self-controlled and alert. Your enemy prowls around like a lion looking for someone to devour. Resist him, standing firm in the faith." (1 Peter 5:8–9 NIV)
- "No weapon formed against you will prosper; and each tongue that accuses you in judgment you will condemn. This is the heritage of the Lord, and the vindication is from me, declares the Lord." (Isaiah 54:17, NIV)
- "Put on the full armor of God, so that you can stand against the devil's scheme. For our struggle is not against flesh and blood, but against the ruler, against the authorities, against the power of the dark world and against the spiritual forces of evil in the heavenly realms. Therefore put on the full armor of God, so that when the day of evil comes, you may be able to stand your ground, and after you have done everything to stand. Stand firm then, with the belt of truth buckled around your waist with the breastplate of righteousness in place, and with flaming of evil one, take the helmet of salvation and the sword of the Spirit, which is the word of God." (Ephesians 6:11–17 NIV)
- "In all these things, we are more than conquerors through Him that loved us." (Romans 8:37 NIV)

- "But thanks to God who gives us victory through our Lord Jesus Christ." (1 Corinthians 15:57 NIV)
- "Not by might nor by power, but by my spirit, says the Lord of hosts." (Zechariah 4:6 NIV)
- "But the Lord is faithful, and he will strengthen you and protect you from the evil one." (2 Thessalonians 3:3 NIV)
- "The Lord will cause your enemies who rise against you to be defeated before you. They shall come out against you one way and flee before you seven ways." (Deuteronomy 28:7 NIV)
- "I have told you these things, so that in me you may have peace. In this world you will have trouble. But take heart! I have overcome the world." (John 16:33 NIV)
- "You will keep in perfect peace those whose minds are steadfast, because they trust in you." (Isaiah 26:3 NIV)

Before I end this book, I just want to ask, "Do you know this Jesus Christ, our Redeemer?" If you do not know Him, I want to offer you a chance to ask Him into your heart to save you. You can ask Him to save you from all your sins, no matter how badly you have sinned. He will forgive you and save you to live forever. Just pray a prayer in your heart, something like this:

> Lord Jesus, I am sorry for my sins, and I need You to save me. Please come into my heart, and save me from eternal punishment. I will turn from my sins and through faith turn to You. Lord, I will trust You to save me, and I will live for You and read my Bible. When the pandemic is over, I will join in worship with a community of believers so I can have a stronger walk with You. If I am not able to join them in person, I will join them online. Lord, thank You for saving me. I do not take Your sacrifice of death for me lightly. I love You and will follow You all my days. In Jesus's name I pray, Amen.

If you prayed that prayer, the silent enemy will try to make you feel like it never happened. Do not listen to him; he is a liar. It is through faith and the word of our testimony on the day we stand with Jesus before God that we are redeemed. John 3:16 says, "For God so loved the world, that he gave his only begotten Son, that whosoever believeth in him should not perish, but have everlasting life." So always trust what your Bible tells you. I encourage you to love your faith leaders. They are not perfect, but the Lord put them in your path for a purpose, so pray for them as they teach you. If you hold any grudges, forgive them quickly so that you can heal inside. Do not hold grudges; they will destroy you. Give them over to the Lord. God will take care of your enemies, friends, and faith leaders. He will avenge them, so just trust in Him. The Bible says, "Dearly beloved, avenge not yourselves, but rather give place unto wrath: for it is written, Vengeance is mine; I will repay, saith the Lord" (Romans 12:19). The scripture continues, "On the contrary: 'If your enemy is hungry, feed him; if he is thirsty, give him something to drink. In doing this, you will heap burning coals on his head'" (Romans 12:20 NIV). I'm reminding you that the silent enemy is the devil, and he wants everyone to be enemies. Do not fall prey to his lies. The Lord says to try to strive with your brother in peace. Romans 12:18 says if possible, strive with everyone in peace. "If it is possible, as far as it depends on you, live at peace with everyone" (Romans 12:18 NIV).

I leave you with two verses and a song that rings in my ears that one of my former pastors always encouraged us to remember as we served in his ministry and often sang in his church. The song is the "God of the Mountain," and the pastor is Ralph Sexton (https://ralphsextonministries.com/) from Asheville, North Carolina. The song reminds us that "the God of the mountain is still God of the valley, and when things go wrong He will make them right!"[60]

I'd like to tell my testimony of my protection by the Lord. I experienced this when I was in my thirties. I was the backup singer in Jesus is the Voice of Reason. We were supposed to go on three cable stations in Nashville when I had an encounter with the Lord and was struck down for my witness. I encountered the Lord, and He showed me a vision of the Pearly Gates. The near-death experience I went through, in which God protected me, alludes to this scripture:

> He who dwells in the secret place of the Most
> High
> Shall abide under the shadow of the Almighty.
> I will say of the Lord, "He is my refuge and
> my fortress;
> My God, in Him I will trust."
> Surely He shall deliver you from the snare of
> the fowler
> And from the perilous pestilence.
> He shall cover you with His feathers,
> And under His wings you shall take refuge;
> His truth shall be your shield and buckler.
> You shall not be afraid of the terror by night,

Nor of the arrow that flies by day,
Nor of the pestilence that walks in darkness,
Nor of the destruction that lays waste at
noonday. (Psalm 91:1–6 NKJV)

Through this experience I know He is real and will protect us, His children.

Retired pastor James Lamb, also from western North Carolina, my childhood pastor, and the former pastor where I served in ministry with my children, recited this scripture at the end of many worship services we attended: "Now unto him that is able to keep you from falling, and to present you faultless before the presence of his glory with exceeding joy, to the only wise God our Savior, be glory and majesty, dominion and power, both now and forever. Amen" (Jude 24–25).

Lord, I am writing this book to help our dear president and faithful leaders to fight against this silent enemy" and to bring solace to the families that suffered from this horrible pandemic. Lord, I wish to help those who suffer to own a Bible. Lord, please help me to send Bibles to all who suffered and to those who need them. Lord, may all faith leaders join me in this outreach and vision so we can help others.

"But his delight is in the law of the Lord; and in his law doth he meditate day and night" (Psalm 1:2). You see, we must get the Word of God to the people, so they can meditate on it day and night. God will hear our prayers and our land. I pray all leaders will help me in this outreach so it can truly be said we keep America faithful." And may God bless America is my earnest prayer.

CHAPTER NOTES

Introduction

[1] The scripture 2 Chronicles 7:14 (KJV) is the basis of the Keeping America Faithful movement and our attempts to provide survivors and their families with Bibles during the COVID-19 pandemic.

Chapter 1

[2] David Jeremiah, "A Warriors Prayer: How to Pray when Satan Attacks," Crosswalk.com *Turning Point* (October 19, 2018), https://www.crosswalk.com/faith/prayer/a-warrior-s-prayer-how-to-pray-when-satan-attacks.html.

3   Joyce Meyer, *Battlefield of the Mind: Winning the Battle in Your Mind* (Tulsa, OK: Harrison House, 1995), 11.

4   Meyer, *Battlefield of the Mind*.

5   Greg Laurie, "How to Stand Strong through the Devil's Attacks," Harvest Ministries, https://harvest.org/know-god-article/how-to-stand-strong-through-the-devils-attacks/.

6   Laurie, "How to Stand Strong through the Devil's Attacks."

7   Laurie, "How to Stand Strong through the Devil's Attacks."

8   Laurie, "How to Stand Strong through the Devil's Attacks."

9   Laurie, "How to Stand Strong through the Devil's Attacks."

10   Laurie, "How to Stand Strong through the Devil's Attacks."

11   Laurie, "How to Stand Strong through the Devil's Attacks."

12   Moriah Balingit and Ariaina Eunjung Cha, "Trump Administration Moves to Protect Prayer in Public Schools and Federal Funds for Religious Organizations," *Washington Post*, January 16, 2020, https://www.washingtonpost.com/education/2020/01/16/trump-administration-moves-protect-prayer-public-schools-federal-funds-religious-organizations/.

13   Megan Trimble, "Trump Appears to Support Bible Literacy Bills: Christian Lawmakers Are Pushing a Half-Dozen Bills to Teach Bible Literacy in Schools," *U.S. News & World Report*, January 28, 2019, https://www.usnews.com/news/national-news/articles/2019-01-28/president-donald-trump-appears-to-support-school-bible-literacy-bills-in-tweet.

14   History.com Editors, "This Date in History: The Pilgrims," The History Channel, December 2, 2009; last modified November 21, 2019, https://www.history.com/topics/colonial-america/pilgrims.

Chapter 2

15   Ryan Foley, "Pres. Trump Adds March for Life Founder Nellie Gray to National Garden of Heroes," *Christian Post*, January 19, 2021, https://www.christianpost.com/news/trump-adds-march-for-life-founder-nellie-gray-to-national-garden-of-heroes.html.

16   Foley, "Pres. Trump Adds March for Life Founder Nellie Gray to National Garden of Heroes."

17   *The Hill* Staff, "Full Speech: Addressing March for Life, Trump Touts Gains in Anti-Abortion Policy," *The Hill*, January 19, 2018, https://thehill.com/opinion/whitehouse/369761-full-speech-addressing-march-for-life-trump-touts-advances-in-anti.

18   *The Hill* Staff, "Full Speech: Addressing March for Life, Trump Touts Gains in Anti-Abortion Policy."

19   *The Hill* Staff, "Full Speech: Addressing March for Life, Trump Touts Gains in Anti-Abortion Policy."

20   *The Hill* Staff, "Full Speech: Addressing March for Life, Trump Touts Gains in Anti-Abortion Policy."

21   *The Hill* Staff, "Full Speech: Addressing March for Life, Trump Touts Gains in Anti-Abortion Policy."

22 *The Hill* Staff, "Full Speech: Addressing March for Life, Trump Touts Gains in Anti-Abortion Policy."

23 *The Hill* Staff, "Full Speech: Addressing March for Life, Trump Touts Gains in Anti-Abortion Policy."

24 *The Hill* Staff, "Full Speech: Addressing March for Life, Trump Touts Gains in Anti-Abortion Policy."

25 "Declaration of Independence: A Transcription," July 4, 1776, *America's Founding Documents*, National Archives and Records Administration, accessed January 24, 2021, https://www.archives.gov/founding-docs/declaration-transcript.

Chapter 3

26 *The Hill* Staff, "Full Speech: Addressing March for Life, Trump Touts Gains in Anti-Abortion Policy."

27 Bishop Joseph Mattera, "7 Powerful Traits of the Joshua Generation," *Christ Covenant Coalition* (blog), February 6, 2017, http://www.christcovenantcoalition.com/blog-entries/2017/2/6/7-powerful-traits-of-the-joshua-generation.

28 "Trump Cuts New Hampshire Rally Short to Receive Remains of 2 Soldiers Killed in Afghanistan," Fox News, February 10, 2020, https://www.foxnews.com/politics/trump-cuts-new-hampshire-rally-short-to-receive-remains-of-2-soldiers-killed-in-afghanistan.

29   Tom Howell Jr., "Trump Flies to Dover after Rally to Pay Respects to Two Soldiers Killed in Afghanistan," *The Washington Times*, February 10, 2020, https://www.washingtontimes.com/news/2020/feb/10/trump-flies-dover-javier-gutierrez-antonio-rodrigu/.

Chapter 4

30   Jonah Valdez, "President Trump to View Riverside Harvest Church's Streaming Palm Sunday Service," *The Press-Enterprise*, April 4, 2020, https://www.pe.com/2020/04/04/president-trump-to-view-riverside-harvest-churchs-streaming-palm-sunday-service/.

31   Valdez, "President Trump to View Riverside Harvest Church's Streaming Palm Sunday Service."

32   "President Trump Joins in Easter Blessing from Oval Office: 'We Place Our Trust in the Hands of Almighty God,'" CBN News, April 10, 2020, https://www1.cbn.com/cbnnews/us/2020/april/president-trump-joins-in-easter-blessing-from-oval-office-we-place-our-trust-in-the-hands-of-almighty-god.

33   "President Trump Joins in Easter Blessing from Oval Office."

34   "President Trump Joins in Easter Blessing from Oval Office."

Chapter 5

[35]   Tiffany Jothen, "Franklin Graham, Michael W. Smith to Share Easter Message from NYC," *Stories*, Billy Graham Evangelistic Association, April 8, 2020, https://billygraham.org/story/franklin-graham-to-share-easter-message-from-nyc/.

[36]   Fox News, "Rev. Franklin Graham's Easter Sunday Message," April 12, 2020, video, 28:45, https://video.foxnews.com/v/6148889517001#sp=show-clips.

[37]   "Begin Your Journey to Peace," Billy Graham Evangelistic Association, 2021, PeaceWithGod.net, http://peacewithgod.net/?utm_source=bgmainsite&utm_medium=link&utm_campaign=pwg+internal&utm_content=His%20love&outreach=His%20love.

[38]   Billy Graham, "My Neighbor Claims to Be a Christian, But He's about the Most Negative and Critical Person I know. Jesus Wasn't Like This, Was He?" *Answers* (Selection of answers originally published in Billy Graham's *My Answer* column), Billy Graham Evangelistic Association, September 27, 2016, https://billygraham.org/answer/was-jesus-like-my-christian-neighbor-negative-and-critical/.

Chapter 6

[39]   "Be Best: First Lady Melania Trump's Initiative," The White House, last updated January 18, 2021, https://trumpwhitehouse.archives.gov/bebest/.

Chapter 7

[40] Charlie Hall, "Second Lady Pence Visits Camp Lejeune, Offers Support to Military Spouses," *JD News* (*Jacksonville Daily News*), January 30, 2020, https://www.jdnews.com/news/20200130/second-lady-pence-visits-camp-lejeune-offers-support-to-military-spouses.

[41] "Second Lady Karen Pence's Efforts to Raise Awareness on Licensing Reform for Military Spouses," The White House, October 22, 2020, https://trumpwhitehouse.archives.gov/briefings-statements/second-lady-karen-pences-efforts-raise-awareness-licensing-reform-military-spouses/.

[42] Charlie Hall, "Second Lady Pence Visits Camp Lejeune, Offers Support to Military Spouses."

Chapter 8

[43] Jeanine Santucci, "What We Know about the White House Coronavirus Task Force Now That Mike Pence Is in Charge," *USA Today*, February 27, 2020, updated February 28, 2020, https://www.usatoday.com/story/news/politics/2020/02/27/coronavirus-what-we-know-mike-pence-and-task-force/4891905002/.

44 Grace Hauck, "The First US Case. The First Death. The First Outbreak at a Nursing Home," *USA Today*, January 19, 2021, https://www.usatoday.com/in-depth/news/nation/2021/01/19/first-covid-case-us-year-anniversary-snohomish-county/4154942001/.

45 Allison Aubrey, "Trump Declares Coronavirus a Public Health Emergency and Restricts Travel from China," NPR WUOT 91.9 FM, January 31, 2020, https://www.npr.org/sections/health-shots/2020/01/31/801686524/trump-declares-coronavirus-a-public-health-emergency-and-restricts-travel-from-c.

46 Alexander Bolton, "GOP Senators Tell Trump to Make Fauci Face of Government's Coronavirus Response," *The Hill*, March 10, 2020, https://thehill.com/homenews/senate/486870-gop-senators-tell-trump-to-make-fauci-face-of-governments-coronavirus.

47 HHS Press Office, "Trump Administration Distributes Incentive Payments to Nursing Homes Curbing COVID-19 Deaths and Infections," US Department of Health and Human Services, October 28, 2020, https://www.hhs.gov/about/news/2020/10/28/trump-administration-distributes-incentive-payments-to-nursing-homes-curbing-covid-19-deaths-and-infections.html.

48 Charles Stanley, "Strength for the Fearful," *In Touch* Ministries, May 29, 2019, https://www.intouch.org/read/magazine/daily-devotions/strength-for-the-fearful.

49 Tony Evans, "Tony Evans Shares on How to Stay Calm in a Crisis," March 19, 2020, video, 6:59, https://youtu.be/TO9Z8XL3M0k.

50 Joseph Prince, *Unmerited Favor* (Lake Mary, FL: Charisma House, 2010).

Chapter 9

51 *Decision Magazine* Staff, "I Knew God Wouldn't Forget Me: Andrew and Norine Brunson Tell How God Sustained Them during Andrew's Two Years in Prison," *Decision Magazine*, Billy Graham Evangelistic Association, December 1, 2018, https://decisionmagazine.com/knew-god-wouldnt-forget-me/.

Chapter 10

52 John and Matt Hagee, "Storm Proof," Hagee Ministries, June 16, 2020, video, 32:43, https://youtu.be/OevavsK1yyE.

53 John Hagee, *Storm Proof* (South Lake, TX: Improve, Ltd, 2019), 152.

54 Marilyn Hickey and Sarah Bowling, "Marilyn & Sarah," Marilyn Hickey Ministries, 2021, https://www.marilynandsarah.org/.

55 Marilyn Hickey, "Satan Proof Your Home," ad, Marilyn Hickey Ministries, accessed March 11, 2021, https://marilynandsarah.netviewshop.com/shopdetail/sphu.

56 "Bible Verses about the Spirit," DailyVerses.net, https://dailyverses.net/spirit/kjv.

57 Max Lucado, "Online Church with Max Lucado Featuring Steven Curtis Chapman," May 3, 2020, Facebook, video, 10:18, https://www.facebook.com/maxlucado/videos/297474914602525/?sfnsn=mo.

Chapter 11

58 Debbie McDaniel, "31 Spiritual Warfare Scriptures: Help for Facing Life's Battles," Crosswalk.com, *Blogs*, March 2, 2021, https://www.crosswalk.com/blogs/debbie-mcdaniel/31-spiritual-warfare-scriptures.html#.

59 McDaniel, "31 Spiritual Warfare Scriptures: Help for Facing Life's Battles."

60 Gaither Music TV, "Bill & Gloria Gaither—God on the Mountain [Live] ft. Lily Weatherford," November 15, 2012, video, 3:23, https://youtu.be/J_mw33Fql9I.

BIBLIOGRAPHY

Aubrey, Allison. "Trump Declares Coronavirus a Public Health Emergency and Restricts Travel from China." NPR WUOT 91.9 FM. January 31, 2020. https://www. npr.org/sections/health-shots/2020/01/31/801686524/ trump-declares-coronavirus-a-public-health-emergency-and-restricts-travel-from-c.

Balingit, Moriah, and Ariaina Eunjung Cha. "Trump Administration Moves to Protect Prayer in Public Schools and Federal Funds for Religious Organizations." *Washington Post,* January 16, 2020. https://www. washingtonpost.com/education/2020/01/16/trump-administration-moves-protect-prayer-public-schools-federal-funds-religious-organizations/.

"Be Best: First Lady Melania Trump's Initiative." The White House. Last updated January 18, 2021. https://trumpwhitehouse.archives.gov/bebest/.

"Begin Your Journey to Peace." Billy Graham Evangelistic Association, 2021. PeaceWithGod.net. http://peacewithgod.net/?utm_source=bgmainsite&utm_medium=link&utm_campaign=pwg+internal&utm_content=His%20love&outreach=His%20love.

"Bible Verses about the Spirit." DailyVerses.net. https://dailyverses.net/spirit/kjv.

Bolton, Alexander. "GOP Senators Tell Trump to Make Fauci Face of Government's Coronavirus Response." *The Hill*, March 10, 2020. https://thehill.com/homenews/senate/486870-gop-senators-tell-trump-to-make-fauci-face-of-governments-coronavirus.

Decision Magazine Staff. "I Knew God Wouldn't Forget Me: Andrew and Norine Brunson Tell How God Sustained Them during Andrew's Two Years in Prison." Interviewed by Jim Dailey. *Decision Magazine*, December 1, 2018. Billy Graham Evangelistic Association. https://decisionmagazine.com/knew-god-wouldnt-forget-me/.

"Declaration of Independence: A Transcription." (July 4, 1776.) *America's Founding Documents*. National Archives and Records Administration. Accessed January 24, 2021. https://www.archives.gov/founding-docs/declaration-transcript.

Evans, Tony. "Tony Evans Shares on How to Stay Calm in a Crisis." March 19, 2020. Video, 6:59. https://youtu.be/TO9Z8XL3M0k.

Foley, Ryan. "Pres. Trump Adds March for Life Founder Nellie Gray to National Garden of Heroes." *Christian Post*, January 19, 2021. https://www.christianpost.com/news/trump-adds-march-for-life-founder-nellie-gray-to-national-garden-of-heroes.html.

Fox News. "Rev. Franklin Graham's Easter Sunday Message." April 12, 2020. Video, 28:45. https://video.foxnews.com/v/6148889517001#sp=show-clips.

Gaither Music TV. "Bill & Gloria Gaither—God on the Mountain [Live] ft. Lily Weatherford." November 15, 2012. Video, 3:23. https://youtu.be/J_mw33Fql9I.

Graham, Billy. "My Neighbor Claims to Be a Christian, But He's about the Most Negative and Critical Person I Know. Jesus Wasn't Like This, Was He?" *Answers* (Selection of answers originally published in Billy Graham's *My Answer* column.] Billy Graham Evangelistic Association, September 27, 2016. https://billygraham.org/answer/was-jesus-like-my-christian-neighbor-negative-and-critical/.

Hagee, John. *Storm Proof.* (South Lake, TX: Improve, Ltd, 2019).

Hagee, John, and Matt Hagee. "Storm Proof." Hagee Ministries. June 16, 2020. Video, 32:43. https://youtu.be/OevavsK1yyE.

Hall, Charlie. "Second Lady Pence Visits Camp Lejeune, Offers Support to Military Spouses." *JD News* (*Jacksonville Daily News*), January 30, 2020. https://www.jdnews.com/news/20200130/second-lady-pence-visits-camp-lejeune-offers-support-to-military-spouses.

Hauck, Grace Hauck. "The First US Case. The First Death. The First Outbreak at a Nursing Home." *USA Today*, January 19, 2021. https://www.usatoday.com/in-depth/news/nation/2021/01/19/first-covid-case-us-year-anniversary-snohomish-county/4154942001/.

HHS Press Office. "Trump Administration Distributes Incentive Payments to Nursing Homes Curbing COVID-19 Deaths and Infections." US Department of Health & Human Services, October 28, 2020. https://www.hhs.gov/about/news/2020/10/28/trump-administration-distributes-incentive-payments-to-nursing-homes-curbing-covid-19-deaths-and-infections.html.

Hickey, Marilyn. "Satan Proof Your Home." Ad. Marilyn Hickey Ministries. Accessed March 11, 2021. https://marilynandsarah.netviewshop.com/shopdetail/sphu.

Hickey, Marilyn, and Sarah Bowling. "Marilyn & Sarah." Marilyn Hickey Ministries, 2021. https://www.marilynandsarah.org/.

The Hill Staff. "Full Speech: Addressing March for Life, Trump Touts Gains in Anti-Abortion Policy." *The Hill*, January 19, 2018. https://thehill.com/opinion/white-house/369761-full-speech-addressing-march-for-life-trump-touts-advances-in-anti.

History.com Editors. "This Date in History: The Pilgrims." The History Channel. Published December 2, 2009. Last modified November 21, 2019. https://www.history.com/topics/colonial-america/pilgrims.

Howell, Tom, Jr. "Trump Flies to Dover after Rally to Pay Respects to Two Soldiers Killed in Afghanistan." *The Washington Times*, February 10, 2020. https://www.washingtontimes.com/news/2020/feb/10/trump-flies-dover-javier-gutierrez-antonio-rodrigu/.

Jeremiah, David. "A Warrior's Prayer: How to Pray When Satan Attacks." Crosswalk.com. *Turning Point*, October 19, 2018. https://www.crosswalk.com/faith/prayer/a-warrior-s-prayer-how-to-pray-when-satan-attacks.html.

Jothen, Tiffany. "Franklin Graham, Michael W. Smith to Share Easter Message from NYC." *Stories.* Billy Graham Evangelistic Association, April 8, 2020. https://billygraham.org/story/franklin-graham-to-share-easter-message-from-nyc/.

Laurie, Greg. "How to Stand Strong through the Devil's Attacks." Harvest Ministries. https://harvest.org/know-god-article/how-to-stand-strong-through-the-devils-attacks/.

Lucado, Max. "Online Church with Max Lucado Featuring Steven Curtis Chapman." May 3, 2020. Facebook. Video, 10:18. https://www.facebook.com/maxlucado/videos/297474914602525/?sfnsn=mo.

Mattera, Bishop Joseph, "7 Powerful Traits of the Joshua Generation." *Christ Covenant Coalition* (blog), February 6, 2017. http://www.christcovenantcoalition.com/blog-entries/2017/2/6/7-powerful-traits-of-the-joshua-generation.

McDaniel, Debbie. "31 Spiritual Warfare Scriptures: Help for Facing Life's Battles." Crosswalk.com, *Blogs*, March 2, 2021. https://www.crosswalk.com/blogs/debbie-mcdaniel/31-spiritual-warfare-scriptures.html#.

Meyer, Joyce. *Battlefield of the Mind: Winning the Battle in Your Mind*. Tulsa, OK: Harrison House, 1995.

"President Trump Joins in Easter Blessing from Oval Office: 'We Place Our Trust in the Hands of Almighty God.'" CBN News, April 10, 2020. https://www1.cbn.com/ cbnnews/us/2020/april/president-trump-joins-in-easter-blessing-from-oval-office-we-place-our-trust-in-the-hands-of-almighty-god.

Prince, Joseph. *Unmerited Favor*. Lake Mary, FL: Charisma House, 2010.

Santucci, Jeanine. "What We Know about the White House Coronavirus Task Force Now that Mike Pence Is in Charge." *USA Today*, February 27, 2020. Updated February 28, 2020. https://www.usatoday.com/story/news/politics/2020/02/27/coronavirus-what-we-know-mike-pence-and-task-force/4891905002/.

"Second Lady Karen Pence's Efforts to Raise Awareness on Licensing Reform for Military Spouses." The White House. October 22, 2020. https://trumpwhitehouse. archives.gov/briefings-statements/second-lady-karen-pences-efforts-raise-awareness-licensing-reform-military-spouses/.

Stanley, Charles. "Strength for the Fearful." *In Touch Ministries.* May 29, 2019. https://www.intouch.org/read/magazine/daily-devotions/strength-for-the-fearful.

Trimble, Megan. "Trump Appears to Support Bible Literacy Bills: Christian Lawmakers Are Pushing a Half-Dozen Bills to Teach Bible Literacy in Schools." *U.S. News & World Report*, January 28, 2019. https://www.usnews.com/news/national-news/articles/2019-01-28/president-donald-trump-appears-to-support-school-bible-literacy-bills-in-tweet.

"Trump Cuts New Hampshire Rally Short to Receive Remains of 2 Soldiers Killed in Afghanistan," Fox News, February 10, 2020. https://www.foxnews.com/politics/trump-cuts-new-hampshire-rally-short-to-receive-remains-of-2-soldiers-killed-in-afghanistan.

Valdez, Jonah. "President Trump to View Riverside Harvest Church's Streaming Palm Sunday Service." *The Press-Enterprise*, April 4, 2020. https://www.pe.com/2020/04/04/president-trump-to-view-riverside-harvest-churchs-streaming-palm-sunday-service/.

ABOUT THE AUTHOR

Rhonda Rivera is the founder of Surrounded Ministries. She wishes to become a nonprofit and provide Bibles to Americans who desperately need God's Word. She believes this is the key to fighting off the silent enemy and his evil plans. She is a Christian vocal artist who has sung backup on Millennium 7, "Jesus Is the Voice of Reason," and has produced four albums: *Surrounded (in God's Love)*, *Protejidos (Protected in God's Love)*, *Silent Night*, and *Something Good Is Going to Happen to You*. Currently she is working on a new album and tribute song, "Blessings in Disguise" and a "Trilogy Tribute" to the president and faith leaders.

She holds a master's of divinity degree in Christian education from Gardner-Webb University and a bachelor's in Christian education and worship arts' degree from

Montreat College. This is her first book, and her desire is to get the Word of God to the people to strengthen them in their faith as she shares biblical truths. She asks that people keep her undergirded in prayer as she has suffered much in her body and health for sharing God's Word.

To Contact the Author:
Surrounded (by God's Love) Ministries
rrivera@gardner-webb.edu

ABOUT THE EDITOR

The editor of this book was Mary S. Thompson, a retired theological librarian and electronic theses and dissertations administrator at Gardner-Webb University. Ms. Thompson has edited numerous dissertations and a number of books for North Carolina author and motivational speaker Sebastian Byers. Both Ms. Rivera and Mr. Byers have their own writing styles, which sometimes varies from traditional format or grammar as originally proposed by the editor. These cannot be seen as editorial errors but as the author's prerogative. Ms. Thompson is currently the chair of the Carolinas Theological Library Consortium, has been working on writing and editing articles for the "1000 Women in Religion Wikipedia Project," and plans to complete a book on the gospel of John begun by her father before his death. Ms. Thompson holds advanced degrees from Brevard College, Pfeiffer University, Scarritt College for Christian Workers, and North Carolina Central University School of Library & Information Science.